AROMATI

CW00496158

A Handbook of Aromatherapy and Essential Oils

(A Clinical Guide to Essential Oils for Holistic Healing)

Arlene Tonn

Published by Martin Debroh

Arlene Tonn

Aromatherapy: A Handbook of Aromatherapy and Essential Oils (A Clinical Guide to Essential Oils for Holistic Healing)

ISBN 978-1-77485-104-3

Legal & Disclaimer

The information contained in this book is not designed to replace or take the place of any form of medicine or professional medical advice. The information in this book has been provided for educational and entertainment purposes only.

The information contained in this book has been compiled from sources deemed reliable, and it is accurate to the best of the Author's knowledge; however, the Author cannot guarantee its accuracy and validity and cannot be held liable for any errors or omissions. Changes are periodically made to this book. You must consult your doctor or get professional medical advice before using any of the suggested remedies, techniques, or information in this book.

Upon using the information contained in this book, you agree to hold harmless the Author from and against any damages, costs, and expenses, including any legal fees potentially resulting from the application of any of the information provided by this guide. This disclaimer applies to any damages or injury caused by the use and application, whether directly or indirectly, of any advice or information presented, whether for breach of contract, tort, negligence, personal injury, criminal intent, or under any other cause of action.

You agree to accept all risks of using the information presented inside this book. You need to consult a professional medical practitioner in order to ensure you are both able and healthy enough to participate in this program.

Table of Contents

Introduction

What does aromatherapy remind you of? Sweet scents wafting around, through candles, incense sticks, or bathing in scented bath tubs. But Aromatherapy is not limited to these, though all the above are examples of aromatherapy at work.

As a beginner to this world of aromatherapy, you are bound to have a number of questions – what is aromatherapy, where to begin, how to begin, what are the components of aromatherapy, how to use aromatherapy for your benefit, and what are the risks and precautions that you will need to take.

This book covers most of the questions that you have in your mind when you embark on your journey into this wonderful world.

In addition, if you are already into Yoga or are planning to start Yoga, it would be a great combination for you to associate your Yoga practice with aromatherapy. It has been found that if you associate Yoga and Aromatherapy, you will be able to have an enhanced feeling of the poses that you perform; you will be able to recall the emotions that you feel when you smell the aromas that you use during the poses, leading to a relaxed state of mind.

For your benefit, a section on FAQs has been included where many of the questions that you may have are answered.

A section on products, primarily essential oils and blends has been included; and a chapter on recipes or blends has been included. While I have included about five blends for different purposes, you are free to purchase pre-blended products or prepare the blends by purchasing the individual essential oils and blend them together in the ratio provided.

I believe that after reading this book, you will be armed with enough information to embark on this wonderful journey. A word of caution that I have made in this book, and I will keep repeating till the end, is that if you have any questions or clarifications, it is best for you to enroll the services of a certified or trained aroma therapist. It is always better to err on the side of caution than take the risk of using these oils without proper care.

Chapter 1: Methods to extract Essential Oils

In ancient times raw material, meant for extraction of essential oils, was stored in large alobaster/clay pots. Then the pots were placed on fire for heating and water added to the pots, so that steam could generate. A cloth was put on the mouth of the jar so that the steam could push pass through the cloth. This process soaked the essential oil which was, later on, squeezed and pressed out into a vessel, for being collected. This principle is still in vogue, as high pressure steam is employed to pass over flowers/leaves, so that essential oils inherent within the flowers and leaves, could evaporate. Then the oil condenses, and can be easily segregated from the water.

Principle Methods Used For Oil Extraction

1. Distillation (already explained above)

2. Mn Hue rage

3. Maceration

4. Pressing

Hereunder is given a short description of each method.

Enfluerage

This method is employed to extract oil from delicate flowers, such as rose, neoli, jasmine etc, out which is not easy to extract the essences due to their delicate nature. First of all petals/flowers are crushed between glass-trays (or wooden frames) and then these trays are amounted with some (greasy) (animal) fat until the time the fat is saturated with perfume of the flowers.

Maceration

Under this method flowers are soaked in hot water so as to break down cells of flowers which release their fragrance with the oil. Then the oil purified and finally, aromas are extracted out of them.

Pressing

Essential oils arc extracted by squeezing rivels and peel of fruits (such as lemon, orange etc) into a sponge.

Essential Requirements

When plants and flowers have been harvested, they are required to processed and stored to preserve their freshness, as quality of soil, water, local climate or even altitude (at which they are grown) can favourably or adversely impact quality these yields. Plants and flowers grown on a particular soil and under existing local climatic conditions can vary when compared to their growth on another soil, couplet with other factors.

Use only fresh flowers and plants and store them under hygenic and pollution free conditions, as quality of extracted oil is dependent solely on quality of flowers and plants.

Never by synthetic oils which are not natural and pure. Remember, adulterated oils will either harm the user or their beneficial qualities are depleted. Hence always opt for oils of best quality even if you have to pay extra money.

* * *

Carrier Oils

Essential Oils must never be used in pure form due to their strong actions on the body, or due to severe reactions even. Carrier oils are also known as 'Base-oil' which are generally extracted from seeds/nuts, each type of oil having a specific quality. So, always choose the most suitable carrier/base oil to attain specific benefits, as they enhance effectively and efficiency of the essential oils. Take care that neither the carrier oil nor the essential oil causes any type of reactions on the body, whatever may be the mode of its use. You have to be extra careful when dealing with the patients of heart, respiratory, skin and arthritic ailments, as reactions on such organs are quite phenomenal and speedy.

Cost factor plays an important role in the choice of carrier oils, oils of mustard, coconut, jesamin etc. are quite cheaper than other varieties of oils but while choosing any type of carrier or base oil, consideration of suitability and acceptance by the user, must outweigh the cost factor, as all oils cannot suit all persons alike and it is also true in the case of essential oils too.

All said and done almond oil though costlier, is probably the best choice due to its non-allergic and neutral nature, ft is a common practice to massage tender skin of babies with almond oil.

Following guidelines may be borne in mind while deciding about choice of the most suitable carrier oil.

• Almond oil is the most suitable one due to its non-alergic and neutral qualities.

• For inflammatory disorders, like arthritis mustard or jesmin oil can be blended with requisite essential oils.

• Walnut oil balances the nervous system and acts as a co-ordinator.

• Wheat germ is an anti-oxidant and ably preserve a (blended) mixture.

• In order to relieve Pre-menstrual tension (PMT) and various menstrual problems, Evening Prem Rose and Walnut oils may be ideal.

•   For Cell-regeneration Evening Prem Rose, peach kernel and apricol Kernel oils may be ideal.

•   For Stretch-Mareis Sesaine oil is quite often eulogised.

Caution

Before opting for purchase of a carrier oil, ensure that the same has not be entreated chemically rather the same ought to have been processed naturally. In any case, cold-pressed oil is considered to be an ideal choice.

The types of carrier oils, detailed herebefore, are rich in various nutrients and are said to be ideal for sensitive and dry skins, But almond Oil is still the best choice, even if the same is quite costly.

Chapter 2: Using Aromatherapy: An All-Natural Curative

There are many products that are labeled "fragrance oils" or "perfume oils," but these are not essential oils. Many products have labels that state that they are "made with essential oils" but often these products only contain small amounts of essential oil and are steeped with synthetic ingredients. The United States has no regulations against the misuse of the term "aromatherapy" on product labels. Be sure to investigate the labels of any aromatherapy product to make sure all the ingredients are natural. Aromatherapy products are only and always 100% natural.

Health Benefits Of Essential Oils

Despite their widespread use, little is known about the ability of essential oils to treat certain health conditions. Here's a look at the evidence regarding some of the common health problems that essential oils and aromatherapy have been used to treat.

- Stress and anxiety

It has been estimated that 43% of people who have stress and anxiety use some form of alternative therapy to help relieve their symptoms.

Regarding aromatherapy, initial studies have been quite positive. Many have shown that the smell of some essential oils can work alongside traditional therapy to treat anxiety and stress.However, due to the scents of the compounds, it's hard to conduct blinded studies and rule out biases. Thus, many reviews on the stress- and anxiety-relieving effects of essential oils have been inconclusive.Interestingly, using essential oils during a massage may help relieve stress, although the effects may only last while the massage is taking place. A recent review of over 201 studies found that only 10 were robust enough to analyze. It also concluded that aromatherapy was ineffective at treating anxiety.

• Headaches and migraines

In the '90s, two small studies found that dabbing a peppermint oil and ethanol mixture on participants' foreheads and temples relieved headache pain.

Recent studies have also observed reduced headache pain after applying peppermint and lavender oil to the skin.What's more, it has been suggested that applying a mixture of chamomile and sesame oil to the temples may treat headaches and migraines. This is a traditional Persian headache remedy.

However, more high-quality studies are needed.

•   Sleep and insomnia

Smelling lavender oil has been shown to improve the sleep quality of women after childbirth, as well as patients with heart disease.One review examined 15 studies on essential oils and sleep. The majority of studies showed that smelling the oils mostly lavender oil had positive effects on sleep habits.

•   Reducing inflammation

It has been suggested that essential oils may help fight inflammatory conditions. Some test-tube studies show that they have anti-inflammatory effects. One mouse study found that ingesting a combination of thyme and oregano essential oils helped induce the remission of colitis. Two rat studies on caraway and rosemary oils found similar results.However, very few human studies have examined the effects of these oils on inflammatory diseases. Therefore, their effectiveness and safety are unknown.

• Antibiotic and antimicrobial

The rise of antibiotic-resistant bacteria has renewed interest in the search for other compounds that can fight bacterial infections.

Test-tube studies have investigated essential oils, such as peppermint and tea tree oil, extensively for their antimicrobial effects, observing some positive results.However, while these test-tube study results are interesting, they do not necessarily reflect the effects that these oils have within your body. They don't prove that a particular essential oil could treat bacterial infections in humans.

Other uses of Essential Oil

Essential oils have many uses outside of aromatherapy. Many people use them to scent their homes or freshen up things like laundry.

They are also used as a natural scent in homemade cosmetics and high-quality natural products. What's more, it has been suggested that essential oils could provide a safe and environmentally friendly alternative to man-made mosquito repellents, such as DEET.

However, results regarding their effectiveness have been mixed. Studies have shown that some oils, such as citronella, may repel certain types of mosquitoes for around 2 hours. Protection time may be extended up to 3 hours when it's used in combination with vanillin. Furthermore, the properties of essential oils indicate that some of them could be used industrially for extending the shelf life of foods.

Side Effects

Most essential oils are safe to use. But there are some precautions you should take when using them, as well as side effects you should be aware of, especially if you take any prescription medications.

Don't apply essential oils directly to your skin. Always use a carrier oil to dilute the oils. Remember to do a skin patch test before using essential oils. Since citrus essential oils may make your skin more sensitive to the sun, these oils should be avoided if you'll be exposed to sunlight.

Children and women who are pregnant or breastfeeding should use essential oils with caution and under the supervision of a doctor. You should avoid some oils and never swallow essential oils.

Side effects of using essential oils include:

- rashes

- asthma attacks

- headaches

- allergic reactions

- skin irritation

- nausea

Use essential oils with caution if you have:

- hay fever

- asthma

- epilepsy

- high blood pressure

- eczema

- psoriasis

While the most common side effect is a rash, essential oils can cause more serious reactions, and they have been associated with one case of death.The oils that have most commonly been associated with adverse reactions are lavender, peppermint, tea tree, and ylang-ylang.

Oils that are high in phenols, such as cinnamon, can cause skin irritation and shouldn't be used on the skin without being combined with a base oil. Meanwhile, essential oils made from citrus fruits increase the skin's reaction to sunlight and burns can occur. Swallowing essential oils is not recommended, as doing so could be harmful and, in some doses, fatal .

Very few studies have examined the safety of these oils for pregnant or breastfeeding women, who are usually advised to avoid them.

Essential Oil Dos

• Read labels

Unlike prescription and over-the-counter medications, essential oils are not regulated by the Food and Drug Administration (FDA). The ingredients and percent of oil in each item varies, so it's critical to read the fine print. Some producers even dilute oils with other ingredients.

Your best bet: Study the different oils, including their risks and benefits, and choose a trusted brand (ask your doctor or an aromatherapist for recommendations).

•   Use a carrier oil

Essential oils are potent, so much so that they can burn the skin. If you're working with a pure essential oil (without added ingredients), dilute the oil with a mild oil, such as coconut, almond, or jojoba oil and avoid using oils even a blend on damaged or broken skin.

•   Try a test

Instead of slathering a huge amount of diluted oil all over your skin, start small with a test spot, Dr. Rabizadeh suggests. Wait 24 hours to make sure it doesn't irritate the skin before using it more liberally.

- Pay attention to the point of entry

Oils that are safe when inhaled can be toxic if eaten and vice versa. Only ingest oils that are designed for that purpose and check with your healthcare provider about potential interactions. Avoid applying edible oils to the skin. And don't diffuse oils into the air if you suffer from asthma or allergies.

Essential Oil Don'ts

- Don't overdo it

Oils are potent. Most oils are too strong to use straight. Even a small amount of diluted oil goes a long way. As with over-the-counter and prescription medications, use the lowest possible dose to achieve the desired effect.

- Don't use oils instead of meds

Oils are not a substitute for necessary prescription or over-the-counter medications. Because they're not FDA-approved, there are few studies regarding their safety or efficacy, especially for specific conditions.

- Don't ignore reactions.

Adverse reactions to oils can be mild such as red, irritated skin or severe, such as chemical burns and respiratory distress. And taking oils by mouth, even just a few drops in a water bottle, can boost the odds of a negative reaction.

If you apply or ingest an oil and develop some sort of reaction—even a mild one—stop using the oil immediately and consult a health professional.

- Don't use photosensitive oils in the sun

Citrus oils, such as lime, lemon, and bergamot, for example, can produce a rash or even serious burns if you use them before stepping out into the sun.

Chapter 3: Essential Oil Recipes For Hair Care

Deep Conditioning Blend

Ingredients

- 20 tablespoons of Coconut oil

- 16 drops of Lavender oil

- 16 drops of Rosemary oil

- 8 tablespoons of olive oil

- 8 drops of Geranium oil

Method

1.   Take a small bowl. Add all the ingredients into it and mix it well.

2.   Whip all the ingredients until the consistency is that of a cream.

3.   Apply the cream on dry hair.

4.   Allow the cream to stay on the hair for around twenty to thirty minutes.

5.   Rinse the hair well at the end of 30 minutes. Apply shampoo and rinse again.

6.   Regular application of the conditioner will end up in softer and healthier hair.

Lavender and Lemongrass Shampoo

Ingredients

- 4 cups of liquid Castile soap

- 2 cups of Coconut milk

- 2 cups of Honey

- 120 drops of Lemongrass oil

- 8 tablespoons of Vitamin E oil

- 16 tablespoons of Coconut oil

- 80 drops of Lavender oil

Method

1. Take a glass bowl.

2. Pour the ingredients into it one by one.

3. Mix all the ingredients well and store it in a clean glass jar.

27

4.   Shake the jar well before use.

5.   Apply it on wet hair.

6.   Rinse it well after massaging the shampoo well.

7.   This shampoo gives your hair a refreshing smell!

Peppermint and Orange Shampoo

Ingredients

- 4 cups of Castille soap

- 2 cups of coconut milk

- 4 teaspoons of Vitamin E oil

- 40 drops of Orange oil

- 40 drops of Peppermint oil

Method

1.   Take a small glass jar.

2.   Pour the ingredients into it one by one.

3.   Mix all the ingredients well and store it.

4.   Shake the jar well before using the shampoo.

5.   Apply the shampoo on wet hair. Massage the shampoo into your scalp well. Rinse it properly.

Lavender and Rosemary Hair Conditioner

Ingredients

- 8 drops of Lavender oil

- 16 drops of Olive oil

- 30 drops of coconut oil

- 8 drops of Rosemary oil

Method

1.   Take a small bowl. Combine all the ingredients in the small bowl well.

2.   Whip all the ingredients till the consistency of the mixture is smooth.

3.   Take some conditioner in your palm. Apply it gently on your hair. Allow the conditioner to stay on the hair for around thirty minutes.

4.   Rinse your hair well at the completion of thirty minutes.

Hair growth stimulator

Ingredients

•   20 ml apple cider vinegar

•   100 ml Rosewater

•   12 drops of Jojoba oil

•   4 drops of cinnamon oil

•   10 drops of rosemary oil

Method

1.   Take a small bowl. Combine all the ingredients in the small bowl well. Mix until the ingredients turn into a fine paste.

2.   Take some of the paste in your hand and gently massage your scalp with it.

3.   Use the paste on your hair and massage it at regular intervals for better hair growth.

Chapter 4: Artificial Versus Natural Deodorants

Starting with this topic, I'll give you the things you must know in order to understand what is in between these two types of deodorants and how they completely differ from each other. So first things first, what is an artificial deodorant? It is obvious, right?

An artificial deodorant is made up of chemicals and partly natural ingredient. On the other hand, is the All-Natural Deodorant, well we also know that this is very obvious, it all tells it by its name. These deodorants are all made from natural and organic materials or ingredients in order to make those scented anti-bacterial bad odor removing deodorants.Now that I gave you a head start in today's topic, I will be listing down the things you must know why you should switch from artificial deodorant into natural ones. But first why?

In reality, we can use those artificially made deodorants in general but you might want to know that these deodorants don't work at all for some people, because sometimes their body resists these product's effectiveness.

You might be one of these people and in order for you to have a working deodorant product, you might want to try being all-natural in this situation, what I mean is start researching about certain ingredients you can use in making your own natural deodorant that will perfectly work on your body and can adapt on your sweat glands. So now I will be listing down the reasons why you should use natural deodorants than artificial ones.

1. Artificial deodorants do contain ingredients that can be harmful to your health

So here we are again talking about the risks of using deodorants and antiperspirants. There is a study that proved, using aluminum-based antiperspirants can increase the chance of having an Alzheimer's disease by 60 percent.

And yet the theory of increasing the chance of having breast cancer by using aluminum-based antiperspirants are here again although this claim about cancer is not yet proven, why not just become safe and try to change your old aluminum-based antiperspirant into a not aluminum based one right?

2. Natural deodorants have ingredients that are good for your body

There are natural deodorants that contain charcoal on it, and for you to know, it is not only the natural deodorants that use charcoal but also other cosmetic products. So what does this charcoal do exactly?

It helps absorbs moisture more than you can think of and wait for it, the best part is when charcoal is ingested, it can help you with gastrointestinal problems, can you believe that? Can your recent artificial deodorant do that? There are some plant-based deodorants that can help your underarms to stay fresh and smooth. These ingredients are olive oil, clay-rich in mineral, and Shea butter.

They help make your underarms to become smooth and irritation free. When your underarms do not irritate from the artificial products you use, underarm shaves can last longer. And there are some other ingredients that can help smoothen out razor burns and shrink pores.

The good thing about these natural deodorants is that they don't block the pores in our skin unlike what the antiperspirants do. What these natural deodorant do is they let the good bacteria do their own thing on your skin which is to help lessen the odor.

Because like said previously, it is not the sweat that causes the bad odor, the odor only comes out when the bacteria mixes with your sweat. That's why using natural deodorants can help you get rid of this bacteria, making you smell good.

3. Does detoxification happen whenever you switch from artificial to natural deodorant?

There is one statement that said they don't believe in a detoxification period once you switched from artificial to natural deodorant. They stated that once you use the natural one, it will immediately work on the spot.

But for those first timers in using natural deodorants, they must understand that the effectiveness of it still depends on a person's way of living, the food he or she eats and his or her daily physical activities and many more. You must also take note that an aluminum-free deodorant doesn't stop sweat at all.

Those only with ingredients that are safe for you will just help stop the bad odor but they won't keep you dry for the whole day, I mean, they won't keep you dry at all. Just don't stop the sweating, it is not harmful and like said, the sweat is not the one that causes the bad odor, but the bacteria mixed on it. In reality, sweating is a sign that your body is healthy. Don't you want that?

Based on my study, some said that the best way to make the most out of your deodorant is to balance how much you use it. Some people claimed that one or two swipes of deodorants helped them stayed odorless the whole day. And please keep in mind that unlike the artificial deodorants, natural ones only need small amounts to be applied to your underarm in order to work.

Things You Must Know about the Natural and Artificial Deodorants

Of course, you are here for a reason, and that is to know how does these two differ? What are their advantages on each other, disadvantages? And yeah, you are finding the one that will best suit your situation, or in other words, you are finding what product will work best for your body.

It is common for us that we always find precautionary measures in order to be safe from the products that we are going to use.

Well, in this part of the article, I'll be answering down the most common questions asked by people about natural deodorants and artificial deodorants. Stay tuned, you might find the answer you've been looking for here.

1.   Are deodorants and antiperspirants the same?

For a simpler explanation, the antiperspirants work is to stop the sweat glands from producing sweat, well in reality, not stop at all but reduces its production, while the deodorant, on the other hand, stops that annoying bad odor that lingers around whenever your underarms sweat. Although antiperspirants are also deodorants, not all deodorants are antiperspirants. Think of it as an additional feature for deodorant.

2. So which one stands out?

So starting off, antiperspirants stop our sweat glands from sweating right? I believe that you know sweating is a part of the body's process, and it is a sign of healthiness. Sweating is the body's natural way of ventilation. A doctor said that if you don't sweat (naturally), it is a sign that your body can't or doesn't release the toxins inside that can be harmful to us or it is that you are having a bad metabolism.

The aluminum compound in the antiperspirant is an actual aluminum, and it is the most bothering ingredient this product has. So how does this work basically? These small aluminum compounds find their way to block those cells and pores on the skin thus making it look like your sweat glands stopped from producing sweat.

The use of aluminum products like utensils and other stuff has become controversial over the years, and I think that it goes the same with the deodorant. We must stop using aluminum-based antiperspirants. Because long-term use of this aluminum based product can cause serious damage to our tissues.

There is a study that shows aluminum are neurotoxins and can contribute massively to the production of breast cancer cells (the reason why aluminum-based antiperspirants are linked to breast cancer). Not just that, but it can also make the chances of having an Alzheimer's disease high and can cause toxicity in the liver.

Someone said that the use of antiperspirants depends on the person's need. Although the use of antiperspirants is commonly linked with breast cancer, one person stated that the aluminum compounds in the antiperspirants are too small for our body to absorb it completely and cause serious damage inside.

Because studies are still being conducted about the link of antiperspirants on breast cancer, if they are really connected, or if that antiperspirants really cause estrogen to change causing breast cancer cells to increase in amount.

But in order for you to find out what's best for your skin, I suggest that you look at the ingredients of the product you are going to buy.Look if there are common components that can cause skin irritation, these ingredients, for example, are the following propylene glycol, formaldehyde, geraniol, linalool, carboxaldehyde, benzyl salicylate.

And if you are deciding on what type of deodorant to buy, if it's a roll-on, stick, cream or spray. I suggest using the first three and try to avoid sprays, why? Deodorants are meant for skin, not the lungs. It is better to be safe.

3.   Any tips on how can I switch from one product to another?

Well, made up your mind already in changing up your old deodorant? But do keep in mind that before starting a new one you must know that it will change your body care routine. Some of the natural deodorant users suggest that you detoxify your underarms first right after you get rid of your old deodorant. And I also believe that this is essential, it is because the detoxification will remove the excess chemicals your old deodorant had left on your underarms.

Think of this as a new fresh start, then right after you've detoxified your underarms, you can now start with your new deodorant brand. There is a simple mask you can make right at your house for this underarm detoxification, all you need is to mix up these ingredients with water: bentonite clay, apple cider, and vinegar.Well if you are not a fan of that detoxification thing, don't worry.

There is a statement that said our body has a natural way of detoxification, and yes I think you already know what that is already. Yes, of course, sweating. Being part of the natural processes of the body, there is no need to worry from chemicals harming you.

When you already started to use your all new natural deodorant and noticed that it is not working at all, you might want to try to exfoliate your underarms once a week. To do these, all you need is a washcloth then mix it up with oat flour and then unscented oil like coconut oil, then you're good to go.

Now that some of your questions are answered, now I will be listing down the reasons why you should avoid artificial deodorants and antiperspirants and start using natural deodorants now. Is it already obvious that all thing that is natural can benefit us a lot than those with chemical. But why do we keep on patronizing this artificial product? Is it because it is easy to buy?

Saves us time in preparing our own because these artificial ones are pre-made already? Yes, these reasons are also beneficial, but come think of this, is it beneficial for your own health? For me, I don't think so.That is why the best way to stay healthy, fresh and odor free, is to get rid of these artificial deodorants and antiperspirants and start using pure natural deodorants and antiperspirants.

Don't mind the time for preparation and the ingredients, because in the end it will be all worth it. So here are the reasons why you should give up your present artificial deodorant and antiperspirant.

1. Artificial deodorants and antiperspirants contain harmful ingredients

Yes that is right. It is mentioned a lot in this article, especially the antiperspirant having aluminum on its ingredients. So it is better to stay away from these chemical based products in order to reduce or the best, completely avoid complications in your body.

2. Natural deodorants don't contain any aluminum

Although artificial antiperspirants stop the sweat glands from sweating because of the aluminum ions that blocks it. Natural deodorants, on the other hand, work in a very different and safer way. There are compounds in the natural deodorants that help absorb wetness in the underarms effectively, these are plant-based powders and sodium bicarbonate or also known as baking soda.

3.   The scent of natural deodorants are also natural and chemical free

What does this one mean? Artificial deodorants' scents contain a lot of chemicals in order to create that particular scent.

So imagine now the chemicals that flow right into your body. With the natural deodorants, it is all different, as it provides scent coming from essential oils which are all purely natural.

Chapter 5: A Crash Course on Aromatherapy

What is Aromatherapy?

Aromatherapy is a type of holistic therapy that makes use of aromatic plant extracts to improve one's physical health and emotional well-being. Also known as essential oil therapy, aromatherapy is both a science and an art, with millions of people around the world using essential oils to improve the body, mind, and spirit.

How Long has Aromatherapy Been Around?

Aromatherapy dates back to ancient times when ancient civilizations in Egypt, China, and India mastered the art of adding aromatic plant extracts to healing balms and oils. Aside from medicinal purposes, essential oils were also used in religious ceremonies. Before modern medicine, essential oils played a huge role in everyday life as they were known to have countless benefits.

While history tells us that it was the Persians who discovered the process of distilling essential oils, the first written account of the process was published in the 16th century in Germany. But it would take a couple of more centuries before French physicians started using essential oils to treat diseases.

As modern medicine and chemical drugs progressed in the 19th century, European doctors lessened their use of natural botanicals to treat illnesses. For the next centuries, using natural plant compounds to heal diseases was information that only a few people were aware of. Finally, in 1937, the French chemist and perfumer Rene-Maurice Gattefosse coined the term "aromatherapy" after he discovered that lavender essential oil can be used to treat burns. In 1937, he wrote and published a book that talks about the use of different essential oils to treat an assortment of medical conditions.

How does Aromatherapy Treatment Work?

So, how does Aromatherapy work? Aside from being a form of alternative medicine, aromatherapy can also be offered as complementary therapy. For aromatherapy to work, essential oils are either inhaled through the nose (aromatic), applied to the skin (topical), or taken by mouth (ingestion).

Aromatic

This is the most common way to use essential oils, thus the name aromatherapy. Ever noticed how certain scents make you feel a certain way? That's because our minds associate scents to specific emotions. When you smell fresh baked cookies or pine trees or roses, you're likely to feel an emotional response depending on the memories attached to these scents.

Same goes with essential oils. When you first take a whiff of a scent, the olfactory bulb in the brain processes it and triggers an emotion. So when you inhale an essential oil, even if you don't have any memories attached to the scent, your mood changes.

Topical

Another way that people use essential oils is by applying it to the skin. Because of their unique molecular structure, essential oils can quickly be absorbed by the body through the skin. It only takes around 20 minutes for the essential oil to be fully absorbed and a couple of hours for the body to metabolize the oil.

Since pure essential oils can be quite potent, you need to know how to properly dilute it with a carrier oil before applying it to the skin. This way, you can cover a larger area of the skin without wasting your essential oils. It's also important that you apply essential oils to less sensitive parts of the body as some of them are known to irritate mucus membranes.

Ingestion

Ingesting essential oils, while relatively safe, should only be done under the supervision of a health professional who has extensive experience in essential oil therapy. Since essential oils are highly concentrated, self-medicating yourself with them is not an option. For example, a single drop of peppermint oil is said to be equivalent to 26 cups of peppermint tea. Just imagine what that would do to your body.

It goes without saying that you should NEVER give essential oils to children to ingest internally. If you're not 1000% sure that it's safe, don't risk it. Even if it seems safe, it's always best to consult with an expert before you even think of experimenting with any essential oil.

As you can see, getting into aromatherapy is quite easy. And to make it easier, you can use the following aromatherapy products, or tools of the trade, to get started. The great thing about aromatherapy is that you can use each product alone or combine different ones for targeted treatment.

- diffusers

- inhalers

- aromatic spritzers

- body oils for massage

- bathing salts

- creams or lotions

- hot and cold compresses

- facial steamers

- clay masks

Since each essential oil has its own unique set of properties and effects, you can combine different essential oils to create your own synergistic blend. After all, combining complementary essential oils is the most effective way to maximize the health benefits of aromatherapy.

What's even better is that there are over a hundred types of essential oils that you can use in your aromatherapy practice. While most people tend to use the more popular oils, part of your aromatherapy journey is trying out essential oils that you have never heard of. But before you do, make sure to look up their health benefits, as well as the side effects (if there are any).

You can easily purchase quality essential oils online, or at your local health food store. Since essential oils are still yet to be regulated by the FDA, it's important that you buy your supplies from a reliable supplier. Choose your essential oils wisely and aim for 100% natural if you want to reap all the health benefits.

Aromatherapy Benefits

Because of the rising cost of healthcare, it's no wonder that more and more people are seeing aromatherapy as a fast and reliable form of alternative treatment, as well as an effective preventive measure. Essential oils have a wide array of benefits and uses so whether you're looking for a fast-acting way to deal with stress or you're trying to find relief for a health condition you've been dealing with for years, aromatherapy has something to offer you. Here are just a few of the benefits you can enjoy from aromatherapy.

• Balances hormones

• Acts as a pain reliever

• Reduces anxiety, stress, and even fear

• Soothes headaches and chronic migraines

• Boosts immunity

• Fights infections

- Eases sore joints and alleviates pain

- Alleviates pain and discomfort of labor

- Improves sleep quality

- Improves digestion

- Boost energy levels

- Enhances brain functions

- Boost moods and confidence

- Reduces inflammation

- Quickens wound healing

- Stimulates hair and skin growth

What to Look for When Buying Aromatherapy Products

The only way that you can enjoy the therapeutic benefits of aromatherapy is by investing in quality essential oils. Since the FDA doesn't regulate the use of the word "aromatherapy" on product labels, packaging, and advertising, it's easy to think that all aromatherapy products are equal. Any company can use the word "aromatherapy" on their marketing materials without really using essential oils in their products. This is why you need to keep an eye out for unscrupulous companies that are out to get your money without delivering any real results.

Just because a product is labeled as "made with essential oils" or "made with natural ingredients", doesn't mean that it actually is. Some contain a high concentration of fragrance oils that make the product smell good, but have no therapeutic benefits. To make sure that you're buying the real thing, here are a few things that you need to consider when buying aromatherapy products:

Research the company

Reputable suppliers almost always provide their company history, as well as information on where and how they source their essential oils. Plus points if the company offers detailed descriptions for their product line. Be careful when buying aromatherapy products from companies that are clearly not in the business of manufacturing natural products. If aromatherapy products aren't their main business, there's a higher chance that they're using essential oils of inferior quality or they're sourcing their products from an unknown supplier.

Check out the ingredients list

It goes without saying that when buying health and beauty products, the first thing that you need to do is read the ingredients list. Familiarize yourself with the commonly used ingredients in health and beauty products, as well as synthetic ingredients that you need to avoid. By making reading a habit, it will be easier for you to choose aromatherapy products that won't cause any harmful side effects. As most companies are hesitant to include a list of ingredients on their packaging out of fear that the competition will steal their formulation, you can try approaching them directly via email or their company website.

Don't fixate too much on the labels

Since many people are now willing to pay a premium on all-natural products, companies have started to ride the trend. Just because an aromatherapy product is being marketed as "100% natural" or "all organic", it doesn't necessarily mean that it doesn't contain any additives. Again, the best way to know if a product is safe to use is by reading the ingredients list and doing your own research. Another way that you can tell is by checking the price of the product. Since all-natural ingredients are much more expensive to source and process, a product being sold for cheap may mean that it's not the real deal. If it's too good to be true, it probably is.

Practice caution when buying at fairs or availing limited time offers

Some vendors at craft fairs are still in the process of testing out their own aromatherapy products so even if you get them cheap, you can't really judge the quality until you try it out yourself. While buying essential oils from craft fairs and availing limited time offers might save you a bit of money, it might cost you more in the end. So before you buy, make sure to ask the vendor if you can try. Plus once the fair is over, it's hard to tell if these vendors have product liability insurance to cover any damage that their product line may potentially cause. If you want product recommendations, make sure to ask someone who is an expert on aromatherapy and essential oils and not just the vendor.

As intimidating as it may seem, don't let false claims and marketing hype stop you from enjoying the benefits of aromatherapy. All it takes is time and effort to do your own research, and the advice of trained aromatherapy practitioners.

Chapter 6: How do you use aromatherapy essential oils?

Essential oils can be evaporated in a burner or can be used atopically, that is on the skin. Once they are on the skin they will absorb through it and flush through the blood stream. They must be diluted in some way. One lovely way to allow the oils to do their work is to put a few drops in your bath water. Muscles react to the warmth of water and begin to relax. The skin is the largest organ in the body and when you lie in the bath it means there are thousands of pores which allow the oils to enter the body.

The kneading of the fibres of the muscles warms them allows the essential oils to do their work. For this you must use some sort of carrier, generally that would be some kind of vegetable oil but it could also be talcum powder.

It is usually advisable to use a dilution of one drop of essential oils to 25 of carrier oil, but this is not an exact science.

It is worth noting that the body will take what it needs from the essential oils and the rest is excreted as waste. Since essential oils are expensive commodities it is worth remembering that less is more.

Useful carrier oils for massage are

- Almond

- Sunflower

- Borage

- Jasmine

- Coconut Oils

What is meant by neat?

Whilst the large majority of essential oils should be diluted before they are applied to the skin there are some which can be used neat. This means that they can be used directly from the bottle and do not need to be mixed into something else. There are many different schools about when this is appropriate. Some disciplines of professional aromatherapy use a process called the Raindrop Technique where just one drop of the oil is used neat on the energy centre of the body.

Many oils however are what are called dermal irritants in concentration; that is they will irritate the skin. Some of them can give quite severe burns and also skin discolouration. For this reason using essential oils neat is very rarely advocated.

Here are the exceptions:

Both lavender and tea tree can be used neat on the skin.

Lavender poured neat onto a burn will very quickly take the sting out and stop damage going to the lower layers of skin.

Use either lavender or tea tree neat on a spot to kill the underlying infection and get rid of the breakout.

Lavender neat on the temples will quickly ease a headache. Rub undiluted tea tree onto the inside of the skin to prevent spread of a cold or flu infection.

One other trick is to use lemon neat on a wart or verrucae. This is a very powerful dermal irritant so this must be done with a cotton bud onto the affected part being careful not to touch any healthy skin. This is strong anti viral and will kill the virus within days.

Apart from these few ideas it is best to always use essential oils in a carrier of some kind. Whether that is a cream or lotion, in the bath or perhaps in massage oil, the oils are so concentrated there is little reason for them to be used neat.

What are the different ways by which you may apply aromatherapy?

There is a whole wealth of ways to use aromatherapy oils to bring about healing. Although some of the oils, lavender and tea tree can be used neat (that is undiluted) on the skin the rest require some kind of carrier.

Here are some of the best ways of using essential oils:

1.   Bath

2.   Massage

3.   Evaporated Or Diffused Into The Atmosphere

4.   Creams And Lotions

5.   Compresses

In the bath

By far the most common way of using aromatherapy, this is a great way to enjoy a bit of pampering whilst the oils do their work.

In order to wave their magic wands the oils need to be able to get into the body. When you lie in the bath they can do this in two ways. The first is when the oils warm it causes them to change their state into gas. They evaporate into the steam of the bath and then you can very easily inhale them. They travel up to the brain via the sinuses which are the only nerves which go directly to the brain.

Once there they activate a part of the brain called the limbic system. This is the part which we use to make memories but it also affects our moods. The second way is via the skin which is the largest organ of our body.

When you lie in the bath it gives the oils an enormous surface area to go through. The warmth of the water opens the pores so that the oils can get through very quickly at a number of points. Once they enter into the blood stream and circulate around the body. The heart pumps the oils around and the body creates tiny chemical reactions as it goes.

Inside of the body the muscles also respond to the bath. The fibres relax from the warmth and they open allowing the oils far better access to heal.

The effects of using aromatherapy in the bath are really quite radical and take a very small requirement of oils. Around 5 drops is enough for one bath. The process of the oils entering into the system will take around 20 minutes so schedule enough time really to indulge!

Massage

Many people will associate the art of aromatherapy with massage and the two do go hand in hand. Whilst the essential oils do an excellent job of healing on their own, massage offers a whole new dimension to the healing.

The majority of the strokes in a massage are long and slow. A full body massage will take as much as an hour and a half to perform. The patient must lie still for a long time and relinquish complete control to the masseur. This is incredibly relaxing.

Apart from smoothing strokes there is a requirement for more rigorous ones too. These encourage blood flow to the muscles and increase oxygen nutrients too.

To use essential oils for massage, you will need to use a carrier. Use any oil you have in the kitchen cupboard really but for relaxation you could try calendula or borage oils too. Many therapists will also add wheat germ oil to their mix as it increases the vibrancy contained in the oils and also fills the blend with Vitamin E.

Burning

This can be done by using aromatherapy candles or perhaps evaporators too. An evaporator has a bowl atop a candle usually. The bowl is filled with warm water and a few drops of oil are added. As the oils warm they evaporate into the air and bring about changes to the room. Use them for relaxation or also to help unblock noses.

Inhalations are most useful to either cleanse the skin or unblock congested sinuses.

Fill a bowl with just below boiling water and add your essential oils. Put your face around 6-8 inches away from the bowl and cover your head with a towel. The towel traps the steam around you a little like a sauna and then the oils get to work.

Be careful not to scald your skin though as the steam can become very hot.

The warmth of the steam encourages pores to open and body tissue to relax. This also means that catarrh will become thinner and begin to run.

In the case of skin care opening the pores allows the oils to get into the skin but also dirt to come out too. This is a very quick way to deep clean your skin.

Creams and lotions

This is a very useful way to use essential oils on a daily basis. It is only necessary for the oils to get into the system to be able to do their work. Work on the basis of around a 3 % dilution to a 97% base carrier. Skin care for instance works very well in this way. Consider mixing essential oils into moisturisers or masques, or perhaps for skin conditions such as eczema and psoriasis and ointment base may be used.

This can of course be extended to a whole range of possibilities, talc's, shampoos and gels all come immediately to mind.

How to make aromatherapy inhalations?

An aromatherapy inhalation is an excellent way to either treat sinus congestion or to cleanse the skin.

The oils vaporise very quickly and so have very quick access through the skin. It works in a very similar way to a mini steam room or sauna. To make an inhalation is so easy it is daft! Be aware though the steam is extremely hot and can scald if you are too close to the bowl. It is also not advisable for patients who exhibit high blood pressure as the warmth can bring about adverse reactions.

Pour just under boiling water into a large bowl and add essential oils. Take a large towel and place it over your head so it also comes down and covers the sides of the bowl. Keep your head around 6-8 inches away from the bowl to prevent scalding.

By trapping the steam around your face it forces the pores of the skin to open. Oils can get into the blood stream quickly to do their work. The gaseous molecules of the oils are also able travel up the nose to the sinuses and get to work breaking down the catarrh.

How to make aromatherapy room diffusions?

You may also see aromatherapy room diffusers called evaporators. The effect is the same. The process is to find a way which will allow essential oils to diffuse into the air and bring about changes. Usually this is done to change the mood of the room. You may want to have a serene atmosphere in the living room or one for seduction in the bedroom. Other times relaxation or focus may be the key.

There are many ways to bring this about. Here are some ideas.

Use a bowl of warm water

Often these are built into evaporators which you can buy but you can get the same effect by simply putting a bowl of water atop your radiator. The water stays warm and the oils will evaporate. One or two drops of oil are sufficient here.

Use a tissue

This method is limited as eventually all of the volatile molecules will evaporate and so the tissue will lose is potency. I find it useful however to throw a couple of tissues into waste paper bins to add a residual freshness to the room. Simply put one of two drops on the tissue and allow them to evaporate.

Light bulb diffusers

These ceramic rings are designed to sit on top of light bulbs. They are extremely porous so any oil which you add is simply drawn into the clay. The heat of the lamp in the evening activates the oils encouraging them evaporate and diffuse into the air. It is usually sufficient to use just one of two drops or perhaps dilute in a ¼ teaspoon of water.

Tealights

It is possible to buy tealights which contain essential oils. However if you decide to use a normal candle, simply wait until the wax is melted a little and drop one drop of essential oil into the liquid wax.

Here are some ideas of oils which work well in diffusers:

For relaxation

Lavender, camomile, frankincense, vertivert, patchouli and geranium

For romance

Sandalwood, jasmine, ylang ylang

For merriment

Use bergamot, mandarin or lemon grass (lemongrass and citronella are great for repelling inspects too....think BBQ!)

For focus in study

Rosemary and rosewood

For prayer

Frankincense or Angelica

To unblock sinuses

For sinus congestion choose oils such as eucalyptus camphor, myrrh, galbanum and frankincense. To cleanse the skin use oils such as carrot seed, cypress, myrtle or Oakmoss Eucalyptus

It is also possible to buy electrical diffusers too. These have the added benefit of having no concern about exposed flames.

Chapter 7: How Does Aromatherapy Affect Your Health

Aromatherapy has been around since ancient times – longer than anyone can remember, even. This is why in the early 1900s, researchers became curious and studied them for evidence of their benefits. They were able to find proof of the various health benefits that each kind of aromatherapy essential oil possesses. Experts believe that aromatherapy works like this: your smell receptors receive the scent of the essential oils used in aromatherapy. The receptors then send this information to your brain. These particular scents activate areas of your brain, creating hormones or chemicals like dopamine and serotonin. Rubbing or putting oil on your skin can also have soothing effects on your joints and muscles. Some essential oils have anti-inflammatory abilities which help ease soreness and relieve allergies. Additionally, using massage oil blends is the most popular type of aromatherapy used in spas and some chiropractic clinics. You can also diffuse essential oils to freshen the air in your home. It doesn't work like those canned air fresheners you spray. Instead, it literally cleans the air and leaves its scent in the process. Essential oils have antibacterial properties that allow them to kill bacteria and allergens that linger in the air. It can help prevent allergies which can lead to other respiratory ailments and, well, the need for medicines. Aromatherapy is also used as an alternative medicine to improve sleep, relieve allergies, manage pain, reduce the symptoms of anxiety and depression, and more. Some experts believe that it can do all these things because of its numerous medicinal capabilities. Many essential oils have been found to be antiseptic, anti-inflammatory, antioxidant, antibacterial, antimicrobial, antibioform. Essential oils owe their capabilities to the naturally-occurring chemicals in the plants that produce them. These chemicals protect the plant from predators and act as their support system against bacteria. The essential oils extracted from these plants are therefore highly concentrated liquids that still contain these natural chemicals and compounds. This high concentration is also the reason why they need to be diluted with other natural oils like coconut and olive oil, also called carrier oils. There are also different ways in which these oils can be used without using carrier oils. These include diffusion, direct inhalation, and bath infusion.

Some of the conditions that aromatherapy can help you with include:

• Insomnia

- Chronic stress

- Anxiety

- Depression

- Fatigue

- Muscle and joint pain

- Digestive issues

- Respiratory issues

- Skin disorders

Recipe

Roll on Essential Oil Perfume

This is a more concentrated version that you can roll onto your wrists or neck for some quick and uplifting aromatherapy.

Ingredients

• 10 ml roller bottle

• Unscented carrier oil like jojoba or almond

• Your favorite essential oil blend

Instructions

• Add 12 drops of essential oils to your roller bottle and then top it off with the carrier oil.

• Shake thoroughly to blend and voila, you have essential oil recipe for a convenient roll on perfume.

Calming Essential Oil Blend

With the fast-pace of our modern lifestyle, trying to balance work, family, good health and a social life, most of us deal with moments of anxiety and stress. One option to deal with that is to use essential oils for relaxation and sleep. Or create a calming essential oil blend for diffusers. And let me tell you, if you don't have a diffuser, now's the time to get one. Using a diffuser with different essential oil recipes will freshen your home, purify the air during cold and flu season and create a calm, soothing environment. Did you know that anxiety comes from the limbic system in the brain? And our sense of smell is directly linked to it. That means scent is one of the quickest ways to influence your limbic system to calm down. Here are three great essential oil blends for anxiety, panic attacks and sleep. You want to add anywhere from 6-8 drops of essential oils to your diffuser, so for the blend below I started with 6 and you can add a drop or two of whatever oil you prefer if you'd like it a little stronger.

- 2 drops of lavender, 2 drops frankincense and 2 drops ylang-ylang

- 2 drops bergamot, 2 drops of roman chamomile and 2 drops of lavender

- 2 drops of orange, 2 drops of ylang-ylang and 2 drops of frankincense

Essential oil cleaner recipes

When was the last time you looked at the ingredients on the back of a conventional countertop spray? I'll go ahead and tell you, they're not good. Cleaning your house with most over the counter products is one of the quickest ways to create indoor pollution. In fact, their toxic compounds can cause asthma, headaches and chronic respiratory conditions when repeatedly inhaled.

Homemade All Purpose Cleaner with Essential Oils Recipe

Ingredients

• 1 cup distilled white vinegar

• 1 ½ cups of warm water

• 1 tbsp borax

- 15 drops lemon essential oil

- 10 drops tea tree essential oil

- 10 drops wild orange essential oil

- Glass spray bottle

Instructions

- Start by pouring warm water over the borax and stir until it's dissolved.

- Once the mixture cools, add the vinegar and essential oils and mix thoroughly.

- This essential oil cleaner can be used to clean and disinfect countertops, bathrooms or any other surface!

Soft scrub with orange essential oil recipe

Ingredients

• 1 cup baking soda

• ¼ cup castile soap (something like unscented Dr. Bronner's)

• 20 drops orange essential oil

• 10 drops lemon essential oil

Instructions

• Mix all the ingredients together and store in a mason jar in a cool dry place.

• Use this like you would a soft scrub cleaner. The baking soda is abrasive and the citrus breaks down greases or mold. Just apply it to whatever surface you need, let it sit for 5-10 minutes and then use a sponge to scrub it clean! Make sure to rinse off the residue afterwards.

• This essential oil recipe is great for cleaning surfaces with stuck on grime. Think bathtubs, stovetops or toilets. The baking soda is abrasive and cleans deeply while the orange and lemon work on anything sticky or greasy.

Chapter 8: Purchasing Essential Oils

There are hundreds of places you can purchase essential oils from, both in person and online. They're found in health food stores, beauty supply shops and lately they've even been popping up in grocery stores and large retailers. Perhaps the best place to source essential oils is online, but you're going to want to do a little bit of research before making a purchase. Look for trusted companies that are recommended by other people. Some brands are good, some are bad and some are big unknowns. Essential oils aren't heavily regulated by the government and there's little to no oversight in regards to what's actually in bottles labeled as essential oil, so it's important to properly vet any company you're thinking about using before making a purchase.

Many companies grade their oils, labeling them with titles like "therapeutic grade," "medicinal grade," or any of a number of other terms. Be aware these labels are meaningless in the grand scheme of things because they're made up by the manufacturer in an attempt to make their essential oil brand stand out from the crowd.

The best essential oils for aromatherapy purposes are pure, unadulterated organic oils, but determining whether an oil meets those standards may not be as simple as looking at the label. There are companies out there that take expensive oils and adulterate them, adding less expensive oils, which is bad, or synthetic fragrances, which is even worse, to the more-expensive oils to dilute them so they can make more money. This is a common practice with high-end oils like rose otto oil and isn't a problem when the oils are properly labeled. When a bottle is labeled as an oil blend, it usually means other essential oils have been used to dilute the more expensive oil. Oils labeled as absolute have been diluted with something else. Oil blends are usually fine to use for aromatherapy, but absolutes are to be avoided unless you feel you absolutely have to have the expensive oil and can't afford the unadulterated version. Excuse the pun.

It's always exciting to find a great deal on essential oils, but beware of deals that seem too good to be true. If you know the average price of an oil is high and you find it on sale for a rock-bottom price, it's time to step back and question whether the deal is indeed too good. Oils that are difficult to obtain are always going to command a high price and there isn't much manufacturers can do to lower the price of pure oil. Cut-rate sellers may be adulterating the oil and selling it as pure or they may be selling something completely different than what's on the label.

The Difference between Essential Oils and Perfumes

Since they both smell good, it's all too easy to get essential oils and perfumes mixed up. People tend to want to group them in the same group even though chemically they're very different from one another. Further compounding the matter is the fact that some high-end perfumes do contain small amounts of expensive essential oils to enhance their fragrance.

The key difference between essential oils and perfumes is that most perfumes are made using synthetic fragrances. These fragrances smell good and can often be tailor-made to mimic the scents of essential oils, but the similarities stop there. Synthetic fragrances are produced to keep costs down and the bottom line high, but they don't feature the same beneficial compounds that are found in essential oils. Their benefits stop at the good smell.

Even when essential oils are used in perfumes, they don't carry the same benefits as they normally would because they've more often than not been diluted with chemical compounds. Never attempt to use perfume in lieu of essential oils unless all you want to do is smell good.

Essential Oil Applications

Aromatherapy practitioners deliver essential oils to the body in two basic ways. The oils are applied directly to the skin or the fragrance of the oils is inhaled.

When essential oils are applied topically, they're absorbed directly into the skin and can be used to help take care of skin conditions, aches and pains, cramping and a number of other localized issues. They soak into the skin, where they're picked up by the small capillaries resting just below the surface and are transported throughout the body. Essential oils applied topically don't just affect the area where they're applied. Once they make it into the bloodstream, they benefit the entire body. You can rub the oil blend into a specific area of your body or you can have a partner massage it into a larger area.

Most essential oils need to be diluted with carrier oil prior to application. Add a few drops of essential oil or your favorite blend of essential oils to a tablespoon of carrier oil and blend it in before applying it to the skin. There are only a handful of oils that can be applied neat, which is the term used to denote undiluted application of essential oil.

Another method used to topically apply essential oils is to add several drops to the bathtub. It's best to add them directly into the water stream while the tub is filling in order to disperse them throughout the water column. The essential oil will eventually float to the top of the water and will coat your body as you get out of the tub. This technique is best used with mild oils like lavender oil. Make sure you test any oil you plan on adding to the tub by applying a tiny amount to an inconspicuous area of your body prior to getting into a bathtub with essential oil added.

Diffused or inhaled essential oils take similar action on the body to oils that are applied topically, with a couple key differences. When you breathe the fragrance of essential oils in, tiny particles of oil are inhaled and will land on the soft tissues in your nose and respiratory system. These tiny particles are absorbed into the body and make their way into the bloodstream. Additionally, when you breathe in the aroma of the essential oils, the brain registers the fragrance of the oil and begins to release beneficial chemicals into the body as a result. This impacts your emotional state of mind and can leave you feeling calm and relaxed or stimulated and ready to take on the world, depending on which oils are used.

In order to administer essential oils via inhalation, the oils need to be diffused into the air. The following methods can all be used to get the fragrance of essential oil into the air:

• Electric diffusers. There are a number of commercial diffusers that are designed to break the oil into tiny particles and disperse it into the room. Electric diffusers are effective, but be careful not to use one that heats the oil because it can damage sensitive compounds in the oils.

• Atomizers and nebulizers. These machines are highly-effective because they break essential oils up into tiny particles that quickly fill all but the largest of the rooms. Thick oils can clog up these machines.

• Clay pots and reed diffusers. These simple diffusion tools use porous clay pots or pots with wooden rods in them to diffuse essential oil.

Of course, you can always keep it simple and add a few drops of essential oil to a napkin and hold it up to your nose or you can just open the bottle and breathe the fragrance of the oil in. When using essential oils to help with respiratory conditions, fill your sink with hot water, add several drops of essential oil to the water and hold your face over the sink while breathing deeply.

Other applications of essential oils include adding them to natural dental care, skin care and even hair care products to improve their effectiveness. Blending essential oils into these products allows you to up the therapeutic benefits of the product while making them smell great. Speaking of smelling great, essential oils can also be added to a spray bottle full of water and sprayed into rooms with odors you want to get rid of. This same spray can be used in the fridge to clean and deodorize it. It can also be used to deodorize stinky shoes, backpacks and many other items that smell bad. The best part is it doesn't just cover the smell; it completely eliminates it. A few drops added to the rinse cycle of your dishes will leave them sparkling and smelling great and you can even add them to your fabric softener to leave your clothes smelling fresh and clean.

Safe Use of Essential Oils

Essential oils are the concentrated essences of plants. They seem relatively harmless at first glance, but that small vial you're holding in your hand may have taken hundreds, if not thousands, of plants to produce. It's easy to underestimate their true power because they're easy to obtain and it seems like everyone is talking about them these days. I've seen people hand their teenage kids a vial of essential oil, who then proceeded to pour it onto their arms and rub it in to relieve pain from sore muscles. When I asked what they were using, the girls told me it was a blend of frankincense and a couple other oils. I cringed because this sort of application can cause all kinds of different problems.

When it comes to safe use of essential oils, a small amount of oil goes a long way. For oils that are safe for neat application, a couple drops of oil are all that's needed. Oils that need to be diluted can be added a few drops at a time to a tablespoon of carrier oil to create oil blends that's more than potent enough for most situations. Any more than that and the skin can be burnt, especially if hot oils are used. It may not happen the first time, but wonton use of essential oils can result in sensitization and a skin reaction can occur that precludes the sufferer of the reaction from ever using those essential oils again.

Keep essential oils put away where they're out of the reach of children. Most essential oils are too strong for younger children. If you decide to use essential oils on your older children, it should always be done under your supervision and the oils should always be diluted.

Be aware that essential oils are highly flammable and need to be kept away from open flames.

People who have health problems and/or are taking medications need to consult with their physician prior to beginning use of essential oils. Certain oils can interact with certain types of medication and the reaction could negate or amplify the effects of the medication. Pregnant women should avoid using most essential oils because there are certain oils that can bring on menstruation and uterine contractions. Unless you're sure an oil is safe, it's best to avoid it altogether while pregnant or attempting to get pregnant.

When you add a new oil to your collection, it's important to make sure you research that oil and learn about the potential problems that could arise when you use it. Always start by heavily diluting the oil and testing it in a small area before applying it to larger areas of your body. This is an important step for everyone, but those with sensitive skin need to be particularly cautious. Wait 24 hours after application before applying more oil.

If you're making oil blends, skin care products, bath melts or anything else that requires working with essential oils for a long period of time, make sure you're working in a well-ventilated area. Prolonged exposure to certain oils can have a narcotic effect, and this effect can be amplified if you're in a poorly-ventilated room with little air circulation.

Ingested essential oils can be toxic to the body. If oil is accidentally ingested, contact your local Poison Control Center for directions on the best course of action. I know there are some resources out there that recommend ingesting certain oils, but this is rarely a good idea. The other methods of application are safer and the oils make it into the body without having to pass through the digestive system, where they can be damaged by stomach acids and rendered ineffective.

Chapter 9: The Chemistry behind Aromatherapy

Before our foray into the world of essential oils and Aromatherapy, it's important that you have an understanding of the chemistry behind this science.

Essential oils have distinguishing characteristics that give them different properties, whether they are antiseptic, analgesic, anti-inflammatory, or otherwise. Each of these properties is determined by the chemical nature of that essential oil. To know how to derive the maximum potential from each essential oil, it helps to know the different chemical categories that essential oils are placed in.

Broadly, essential oils are divided into two families based on their chemical structure: Terpene Hydrocarbons and Oxygenated Compounds. Every essential oil is composed of some proportion of Hydrogen, Oxygen and Carbon molecules, which then combine in one of numerous ways to fit into one of the two families. It is important to note, however, that every essential oil may be slotted into more than one of the many categories, based on the properties they exhibit, and their chemical structure.

Let's take a look at the characteristics that each of these families imparts to the essential oils.

Terpene Hydrocarbons

Terpenes are compounds that are a vital part of the chemical structure of an essential oil. It is these compounds that give most oils their antiseptic, antiviral and anti-inflammatory properties. Terpenes are also responsible for de-coagulating blood vessels, as well as restoring tone and structure to muscles and connective tissue.

The following two types are most commonly seen Terpene groups in essential oils:

Monoterpene Hydrocarbons

Monoterpene hydrocarbons are among the most commonly found compounds in essential oils. The main feature of a Monoterpene hydrocarbon is to limit the collection of toxins in your cells. Through this activity, they also help restore the balance of the cellular structure in your body. Monoterpene also act as enhancers, bringing up the potency of other compounds in the essential oil.

These chemical compounds are highly reactive to air and heat, which means that Monoterpene essential oils will have to be stored in airtight, cool conditions. Essential oils with a high level of Monoterpene hydrocarbons include citrus oils such as lemon, orange, and grapefruit, along with others like balsamic fir.

Sesquiterpene Hydrocarbons

Sesquiterpene hydrocarbons are those compounds that provide the anti-inflammatory and antiseptic characteristic to your essential oil. Found in nearly every essential oil, these compounds work by omitting any adverse information from your cellular structure and restoring its original nature.

Sesquiterpene hydrocarbons are also more viscous in nature than their Monoterpene counterparts. This means that they have a thicker texture and are less reactive than Monoterpene. This thicker texture also makes Sesquiterpene essential oils easy to combine with more reactive oils for potent results.

Oils with Sesquiterpene hydrocarbons have found to have a calming, and balancing effect on the mind and emotions as well. Essential oils with high levels of Sesquiterpene include sandalwood, cedarwood, chamomile, rose and myrrh. Oxygenated Compounds

Alcohols

It is the alcohol group of compounds that imparts the energizing or uplifting characteristic to your essential oil. Highly favored in aromatherapy, oils with alcohol compounds are known to have antiviral, antiseptic, and antibacterial properties. The alcohol group also provides a stimulating as well as hypnotic effect to the body, without any side effects or allergic reactions.

Most alcohol-group essential oils can be recognized by their subtle, soft, and often earthy scents. Common examples include geranium, juniper, lavender, tea tree, rose, ginger, vetiver and patchouli.

Aldehydes

Aldehydes are the group that s anti fungal, anti-inflammatory and disinfectant qualities to their essential oils. When used in aromatherapy, oils with Aldehydes can have adaptogenic properties of being calming yet energizing at once.

The use of Aldehydes in aromatherapy requires care and attention to proportions. While extremely beneficial in cures for ailments, they need to be used in highly diluted forms. Potent in small doses, exposure to high amounts of pure Aldehydes may cause allergic skin reactions.

Aldehydes are highly reactive to air and heat. The slightest contact with oxygen or even mildly warm temperatures will bring about a chemical reaction in Aldehydes-group essential oils. Lemongrass, eucalyptus, citronella and melissa are some of the essential oils that belong to the Aldehydes group.

Coumarins and Lactones

Coumarins are the compounds that provide the anticoagulant and sedative properties to their essential oils. Since this compound also imparts its oils with the ability to secret mucus better, Coumarins are highly effective in the treatment of chest-related ailments such as bronchitis.

A sub-type of Coumarins, however, known as furocoumarin, has a highly phototoxic nature. This means that essential oils with furocoumarin compounds become highly reactive and toxic when exposed to long periods of light.

Another group of compounds that is useful in treating chest ailments, yet is phototoxic in nature is a group called Lactones. Lactones also possess anti-inflammatory properties, but can be irritating to the skin upon excessive exposure to light.

Lactones and Coumarins, therefore, need to be used in controlled quantities for short periods of time, and stored away from light. Essential oils that are Coumarins compounds include bergamot, tonka bean, vanilla grass, and sweet grass. Essential oils that contain lactones include jasmine.

Esters

Esters are one of the most cherished among the essential oil compound groups. It is the esters that provide the antispasmodic and relaxing effect to the nervous system and the body. These compounds are formed due to the reactions of alcohols with acids, giving them their calming and sedative properties. The alcohol contribution to the ester group also gives these compounds strongly fragrant characteristics.

Additionally, some ester-group essential oils are have high anti microbial qualities, making them essential in many home treatments. But the feature that makes esters the among the most values essential oil groups is their gentle nature. These compounds mix well with others without bringing about any adverse reactions in the skin. Essential oils with ester compounds include lavender, geranium, bergamot and clary sage.

Ketones

Ketones are those chemical compounds that give their essential oils the ability to enable tissue regeneration and secretion of mucus. These properties are what help your cells and tissue recover faster from injuries and wounds. In addition, treatment with ketones can also help lighten scarring and spots on the skin.

Ketones are a group in the essential oil family tree that need to handled with extreme care. While these oils are highly effective in treatment, they can also be highly toxic. An example of this toxicity is found in the compound Thujone. Found in thuja, which is used in creams to remove stretch marks, excessive exposure to Thujone is known to cause birth defects when used by women.

However, when used in the right amounts and in moderation, kenotic oils have restorative and therapeutic properties that are highly valued. Essential oils with ketone structures include hyssop, rosemary, thuja, wormwood and eucalyptus.

Phenols

Phenols are an important group in the essential oil family tree. These compounds are responsible for a strong fragrance in those oils that belong to the phenol family. Phenol-structured oils are known to have high disinfectant and antiseptic properties. In addition, these oils can also be highly stimulating when used in the correct doses.

The distinguishing feature of phenols is the high number of oxygen molecules they contain. While this makes them effective in improving blood circulation in the body, they also can cause severe reactions when exposed to the skin for too long.

Internally, lengthy periods of treatment with phenolic oils may lead to a toxic buildup, forcing liver damage in the long run.

When used in treatments for a short period in the right amounts, however, phenolic oils can help strengthen and simulate your body and mind, while providing an antiseptic barrier. Essential oils with phenolic properties include cinnamon, clove, wintergreen, thyme and tea tree, among others.

Chapter 10: History of Aromatherapy

Aromatherapy is not a novel concept. In fact, this practice has been in existence for therapeutic purposes since the beginning of recorded history. Ancient civilizations used essential oils mainly for ritualistic, hygienic, and spiritual purposes.

Egypt:

Egyptians can be called the pioneers in practicing aromatherapy. It was a sacred concept for them. At grand religious rituals, the Egyptians rubbed fragranced oil and botanicals onto the statues of their deities to glorify them. They also adorned their bodies with these aromatic oils in order to earn holiness. It was due to this that the body of a deceased person, especially pharaohs, was wrapped in a cloth that had myrrh, cedar wood, cinnamon, and other oils so that the deceased person would smell holy and would be acceptable to their deity.

Apart from spiritual purposes, the wealthy Egyptians perfumed their bodies with these aromatic essences as they believed it would keep their skin beautiful and make them look appealing. Cleopatra is widely eminent for her extensive use of aromatic substances to allure men and to preserve her skin. Applying oil after bathing was common practice for Egyptians as it protected the skin from the harsh climate in Egypt.

China and India:

The ancient Indian civilization used essentials oils for healing both bodily and psychological illnesses in addition to the widespread use of aromatic scents and oil for sacred rituals. The holy text of the Vedas also mentions the miraculous properties of a variety of botanicals, such as sandalwood, ginger, and myrrh. This is what led to the practice of the ancient healing science of 'Ayurverda' in India.

The priests used to burn incense made of sandalwood, patchouli, and benzoin in places of worship as they believed this would cast out wicked spirits. Even worshippers used to anoint their bodies with these scented oils due to their religious beliefs that the use of aromatic plants would help them get rid of their sins.

People of the Chinese civilization also rubbed their bodies with various forms of botanicals, primarily in accordance with their religious beliefs. Burning incense was a popular practice as the Chinese believed it would help create harmony in their lives and banish evil. Moreover, aromatic herbs were burned at funerals as a part of spiritual rites.

Massage therapy for beauty purposes was also very significant with the Ancient Chinese. In fact, this practice is still tremendously popular. Jasmine was particularly used by females who rubbed it gently onto their bodies after a bath. The contribution of the Chinese in aromatherapy, especially with regards to healing medical issues, is also noteworthy.

Rome and Greece:

The ancient Greeks revealed several undiscovered powers of aromatherapy oils, which were until that time only limited for spiritual and religious purposes. Asclepius, the renowned Greek physician, is one of the earliest practitioners of therapeutic aromatherapy and used herbs and plants in various surgeries. Consequently, he was also called the God of Healing.

It is recorded that in about 450 BCE, the father of modern medicine, Hippocrates, elaborated this practice of medicinal aromatherapy further and suggested that aromatic oils must be used by patients with physical ailments, especially those suffering from arthritis. It is recorded that in time of history's worst plague, he decontaminated the city of Athens by fumigation of aromatic substances. The work by Aristotle is also worth mentioning with regard to the extraction of essential oils. Dioscorides was another renowned Greek physician who was widely celebrated for his far-reaching study on herbs in his published work called 'herbarius'. Dioscorides's aromatic remedies are a major contribution in the development of this practice.

Galen, the most prominent Roman physician of that age, is acknowledged to have treated countless wounded gladiators with the help of herbal medicine. Romans are accredited for their innovating distillation techniques that were employed to extract fragrant floral water. Aromatherapy practices were thus elaborated on by the Romans, and Rome essentially earned the reputation of being the bathing capital of the world. The city was well-known for its public bath houses, of which there were as many as one thousand. Visitors received relaxing massages with fragrant oils and botanicals. Largely, the Ancient Romans had their romance with scented oils from natural things, such as the rose, cypress, and fir. They not only loved to abundantly anoint themselves with these essential oils, but they also used these aromatic substances to add fragrance to their homes.

Arabia:

Arabic influence on aromatherapy would be incomplete without the mention of

Avicenna, the Arab physician. His text 'Cannon of Medicine' discussed methods of extracting purer forms of essential aromatic substances, such as rose essence. His contribution to aromatherapy is enormous.

Avicenna's innovation of the use of refrigerated coils in the distillation method and development of steam distillation is, without a doubt, remarkable. Rose oil was one of the most popular essential oils in Arabia where it was used to perfume mosques or was sprinkled on visitors to give them a warm welcome.

Contemporary Aromatherapy:

At the moment, Aromatherapy is enjoying greater recognition and fame than it has ever received in history. It is believed to reinstate an overall sense of balance and boost the quality of life. Today, our lives are becoming increasingly complex, and many of us are living under constant stress and pressure.

General well-being is being compromised, and that can be observed through the rising levels of discontentment, depression, and muscular tension. Moreover, the pollution of environment as well as a dramatic increase in allergic disorders has also caused a lot of people to rethink medicinal alternatives. On the same hand, there is rising awareness among more and more people about the astounding potential of aromatherapy. This is why this therapeutic practice has grown into a popular choice for a lot of people in the contemporary world.

However, aromatherapy as we know it today is an outcome of some stupendous research and discoveries of modern day aroma therapists.

A French chemist, Rene Gattefosse, has the credit of coining the term aromatherapy as it is used in the world today. It is very fascinating to note that his experience with essential oils and their healing effects was a result of an accident.

As a chemical cosmetic engineer, Gattefosse, while performing an experiment, accidently burned his arm. In fright, he plunged his arm into a nearby container containing some liquid. To his astonishment, he saw that the pain had relieved considerably and there were no scars of the burn to be seen. The liquid was lavender oil, which had worked wonders on his arm. It was after this accident that Gattefosse studied the effects of essential oils and performed numerous experiments and studies. He researched various antiseptic and antibiotic properties of essential oils. This marked the beginning of the contemporary use of aromatherapy.

Essentials oils were exceedingly popular during World War II. Dr. Jean Valnet, a medical practitioner who treated injured French soldiers, made use of essential oils. When medicines were scarce, Dr. Valnet used various essential oils to heal the wounds of the injured army men. The results were extraordinary.

Marguerite Maury is also one of the pioneering aroma therapists. She is recognized for bringing the magical wonders of aromatherapy to Britain. She was the first one to develop the exceptional application technique for essential oils – a message therapy which is immensely admired today. She also researched the abundant revitalizing powers of these aromatic substances. She brought her skills and knowledge of aromatherapy to various places by opening up clinics in Britain, Switzerland, and France where she trained many beauty therapists.

We see that the consumers of aromatherapy have wide ranging demands today. For some, it's all about beautification and hygienic functions, while others look at aromatherapy as the science of treating various physical and psychological ailments. And most outstandingly, people have greeted this practice with open arms into their daily lives because of the phenomenal stress busting powers of aromatherapy. People are able to realize their goal of achieving maximum well-being through aromatherapy, which addresses a wide array of problems depending on the essential oil and how it is used.

Chapter 11: How to Create Your Own First Aid Kit With Essential Oils

It's easy to put together a natural first aid kit using essential oils. You can easily treat the same things with your first aid kit built on essential oils, as you can with a typical first aid kit.

Essential oils are a much better choice, because they support your body and let it return to its natural state of balance. They are easy to use and you don't have to have a different first aid kit for the pets or children in your home. Everyone can use this.

Each essential oil has a multiple of properties so it can be used to treat a number of conditions. This means with just 10-15 essential oils as your base, you'll be ready to treat most situations you'll run into.

Of course, in a real emergency, you need to call 911, and get medical help. However, even in these situations, there is a need for emotional support. You need to keep the injured party calm until help arrives and you can use essential oils to help achieve this.

Let's look at the main first aid situations you are likely to face and how you can treat them with essential oils.

Wound Healing With Essential Oils

Healing wounds naturally with essential oils is easy and it's highly effective. Use oils to treat, cuts, scrapes, puncture wounds, etc.

When you use commercial products to treat wounds, chemicals that do not belong in our body are absorbed and this actually can slow the healing process and create other situations like infection.

Many of these products are water based, and the skin repels water, so the product isn't properly absorbed into the skin to promote healing. Ointments and salves are usually petroleum based and that is not helpful for healing wounds. It actually clogs the skin and prevents penetration needed for healing.

Therapeutic grade essential oils help to speed up the healing process because of the combination of medicinal properties. Here are some of the properties you want when you are trying to heal wounds:

- Analgesic (pain relieving)

- Anti-bacterial

- Antibiotic

- Anti-fungal

- Anti-inflammatory

- Antiseptic

- Homeostatic (stops bleeding)

- Vulnerary (helps heal wounds)

All essential oils will have several of these properties, not just one. They have many benefits. Plus, you will be able to address trauma or shock.

Ingredients Found in Commercial Wound Ointments

Here are just a few ingredients that you will find in wound products. Most of these irritate the skin, are linked to allergies, suppress the immune system and some are even linked to cancer.

- Benzalkonium Chloride

- Butylated Hydroxytoluene (BHT)

- DMDM Hydantoin

- Mineral Oil

- Petrolatum

- Propylene Glycol

- Yellow #5; FD&C Blue #1

Sometimes commercially purchased products that claim to be natural will still contain some of these ingredients. Pet products are the worst, because they don't require any labeling.

The Best Essential Oils for Wound Healing

Select the essential oil you are going to use based on the type of wound and the action required.

To Disinfect:

- Tea Tree essential oil

- Thyme essential oil

- Oregano essential oil

- Hyssop essential oil

To Stop Bleeding:

- Helichrysum (The best to control bleeding) essential oil

- Geranium essential oil

- Rose Otto essential oil

To Treat Infected Wounds:

- Clove essential oil

- Myrrh essential oil

To Promote Healing:

- Tea Tree essential oil

- Lavender essential oil

To Help With Scarring:

- Lavender essential oil

- Geranium essential oil

Create a First Aid Spray:

- 10 drops lavender essential oil

- 6 drops tea tree essential oil

- 4 drops cypress essential oil

Instructions:

1.   Place the essential oils in 1 teaspoon of salt.

2.   Put 16 ounces of distilled water in a spray bottle.

3.   Add the salt mixture.

4.   Shake until dissolved.

Spray it on minor cuts, scrapes and wounds before you apply the bandages. You should spray throughout the day several times, for 4 days. You can also apply 1-2 drops of tea tree oil essential oil.

Treat Nausea and Vomiting With Essential Oils

Nausea and vomiting can be caused by a variety of digestive issues including parasites, constipation, food poisoning, motion sickness, indigestion or stomach flu.

There are different essential oils that can help depending on what the cause of your nausea or vomiting. If you are unsure of the cause, there are some general remedies that overlap. That's often a good place to start. However, if you know the cause, then it's better to choose an essential oil that's designed to work in that situation.

General Oils for Nausea and/or vomiting:

• Ginger essential oil

• Wintergreen essential oil

• Peppermint essential oil

- Nutmeg essential oil

Instructions:

Dilute and massage 2-3 drops behind the ear and around your navel area. Do this every hour. You can also use warm compresses over your stomach after you apply your essential oil. You can also inhale the oils as needed. Place 1 to 3 drops directly on your tongue and then swallow the water.

To Stop Vomiting:

- Patchouli essential oil – this is the best because it will

- Lavender essential oil

- Peppermint essential oil

- Nutmeg essential oil

- Fennel essential oil

Patchouli is one of the best oils for vomiting. It has highly effective compounds, because they decrease the gastrointestinal muscle contractions that are associated with vomiting.

Instructions:

Dilute and massage 2-3 drops behind the ear and around your navel area. Do this every hour. You can also use warm compresses over your stomach after you apply your essential oil. You can also inhale the oils as needed. Place 1 to 3 drops directly on your tongue and then swallow the water.

To Treat Morning Sickness and Motion Sickness

- Peppermint essential oil

- Ginger essential oil

Instructions:

Place 1-2 drops in a glass of water and sip slowly. You can also apply directly to your navel area. Dilute and massage 2-3 drops behind the ear and around your navel area. Do this every hour. You can also use warm compresses over your stomach after you apply your essential oil. You can also inhale the oils as needed. Place 1 to 3 drops directly on your tongue and then swallow the water.

To Treat Food Poisoning:

- Patchouli essential oil

- Peppermint essential oil

- Rosemary essential oil

- Tarragon essential oil

Instructions:

Place 1-2 drops in a glass of water and sip slowly. You can apply directly to your stomach area. Dilute and massage 2-3 drops behind the ear and around your stomach area. Do this every hour. You can also use warm compresses over your stomach after you apply your essential oil. You can inhale the oils as needed. Place 1 to 3 drops directly on your tongue and then swallow the water.

Reduce Jet Leg with Essential Oils

When you travel across time zones or body's circadian rhythms get all messed up. This can lead to insomnia, fatigue, headache and mental confusion.

These essential oils along with other techniques can help to reduce your jet lag.

- Geranium essential oil

- Lavender essential oil

- Eucalyptus essential oil

- Peppermint essential oil

- Clarity essential oil

- Grapefruit essential oil

Treating Minor Aches and Pain with Essential Oils

You exercise, you trip and twist something, you lift something too heavy –

there are many reasons why you find yourself dealing with minor aches and pain. Essential oils can help.

Chronic pain, as a result of autoimmune disorders like fibromyalgia or degenerative disorders like arthritis, the relief are more difficult to treat and a combination of essential oils with other natural treatments will give you the best results.

- Wintergreen essential oil

- Helichrysum essential oil

- Clover essential oil

- Peppermint essential oil

- Pine essential oil

- Lavender essential oil

- Ginger essential oil

- Cinnamon essential oil

Instructions:

If you make a blend of wintergreen, helichrysum, clover and peppermint you will get maximum benefits. Lavender disinfects and can also help a wound start to heal quickly along with relieving pain.

Ease Muscle Spasms with Essential Oils

Essential oils work best to prevent injury or muscle spasms, but if you find yourself dealing with muscle spasms, there are some excellent essential oils that work as a muscle relaxer.

- Marjoram essential oil

- Basil essential oil

- Roman Chamomile essential oil

- Wintergreen essential oil

- Helichrysum essential oil

- Clover essential oil

- Peppermint essential oil

Instructions:

Again, making a blend from the last four give excellent results. Mix your essential oils 50:50 with your carrier oil. Apply at least three times a day. You can also alternate between hot and cold packs to increase the relief from strained muscles. Light stretching can also be beneficial.

Essential Oils That Have a Cooling Effect:

- Eucalyptus essential oil

- Peppermint essential oil

- Wintergreen essential oil

Essential Oils That Have a Warming Effect:

- Thyme essential oil

- Marjoram essential oil

- Basil essential oil

- Helichrysum essential oil

- Roman Chamomile essential oil

- Clove essential oil

- Black Pepper essential oil

- Capsicum essential oil

Treat Bee Stings and Bites with Essential Oils

You can quickly and easily address bee stings with essential oils. Essential oils have antihistamine and anti-inflammatory properties that are excellent for dealing with bee or wasp stings. Of course, if you are allergic to bees then you need to seek immediate medical help.

To Treat Bee or Wasp Stings:

- Roman chamomile essential oil

- Lavender essential oil

- Peppermint essential oil

- Tea tree essential oil

Wasps and hornets don't leave their stinger. However, bees do, so if a bee has stung you, first you will need to remove the stinger, and then apply 1-2 drops to the bite. For the first hour apply every 15 minutes and then apply 3-4 times a day until swelling and redness is gone. You can also apply a cold compress.

Because of the alkaline nature of wasp venom, a blend of 3 drops lavender essential oil, 3 drops Roman chamomile essential oil and 2 drops basil essential oil with 1 teaspoon of apple cider vinegar is generally more effective.

To Treat Mosquito Bites Use:

- Lavender essential oil

- Helichrysum essential oil

Another recipe for bites and stings is this poultice:

- 18 drops lavender essential oil

- 7 drops chamomile essential oil

- 1 ½ tablespoon bentonite clay

- 1 ½ teaspoon tincture

- 3 teaspoons distilled water

Instructions:

Mix and blend and then apply the paste to the bite. It helps to remove toxins and provides relief from itching and pain.

Treat Minor Burns with Essential Oils

You can easily treat minor burns at home. However, if you have suffered a major burn, you need to see a doctor immediately. Essential oils do an excellent job of soothing minor burns.

To Treat Minor Burns Use:

- Helichrysum essential oil

- Lavender essential oil

- Rose essential oil

- Frankincense essential oil

- Aloe vera essential oil

Instructions:

Lavender and aloe vera can be applied directly to the burn without reducing with a carrier oil.

Treat Sunburn with Essential Oils

Sunburn is never fun, in fact, it can be quite painful. The sooner you address it the better.

To Treat Sunburn:

- Lavender essential oil

- Helichrysum essential oil

- Tea tree essential oil

- Rose essential oil

These four essential oils make an excellent blend for treating sunburn. There is no question that lavender is the best oil for sunburn relief. It's also important that you draw the heat out of your body. You can do that by making a mixture of:

- 2 cups apple cider vinegar (or white vinegar will work)

- Ice cubes

- 10 drops of lavender essential oil

Instructions:

1.   Fill a bath or sink with tepid water.

2.   Add the 2 cups of apple cider vinegar.

3.   Immerse yourself for 20-30 minutes or as long as you can tolerate.

4.   Once you are in the bath, if you can tolerate the temperature, add the ice cubes to your water.

5.   Gently pat dry.

6.   Now apply undiluted Lavender essential over the burned area. You can also use aloe vera in areas that burned the worst.

Treating Sunburn in Children

If you are treating sunburn in children you can use the recipe above. But you also want to keep your child cool and dry to try to prevent heat rash. Clothing made from light, natural fabrics is best. Expose as much skin as possible to air. If your child does develop heat rash.

Chapter 12: Who Uses Aromatherapy?

Aromatherapy is becoming more widely used in the average household to heal conditions such as anxiety, depression, low energy, and insomnia. However, holistic practitioners (all of whom believe healing occurs in the body, mind, and spirit) are usually the most knowledgeable about the uses of aromatherapy and can often create different mixtures of essential oils for their individual patients. Essential oils are used by holistic practitioners because, while Western pharmaceuticals are meant only to target specific symptoms, many essential oils target specific symptoms but are intended also to bring about a sense of well-being. For instance, peppermint essential oil helps alleviate pain but also conveys a sense of calm.

Aromatherapy has been adopted in medical clinics, hospices, and nursing homes. However, it is not yet a common practice by doctors and hospitals. While aromatherapy has been researched quite extensively in recent years, and while it is known to heal ailments such as viral infections, nausea, insomnia, and anxiety without the need of medications, it is considered more a complimentary therapy by medical doctors rather than a medicine that targets specific ailments. These views are changing, and essential oils are being used more today in clinical therapy.

How Aromatherapy Is Used To Heal

Different plants have many different medicinal properties that are beneficial to humans, and the production of essential oils is a means to target, augment, and take advantage of these properties. Plants themselves contain certain chemicals that they have gained through evolution to repel insects or other animals, to protect themselves against infections, and to heal wounds. The production of essential oils takes advantage of these properties. And while the part of the plant that essential oils are derived from contain medicinal uses, essential oils are exceedingly more potent.

Aromatherapy, then, is practiced in many different ways and for many different forms of health care. Some of these, as mentioned above, include:

- Pain

- Stress and anxiety

- Fatigue

- Burns

- Wounds

- Infections

- Depression

- High blood pressure

- Nausea

- Insomnia

- Inflammation

- Sore muscles

- Headaches

- Skin problems, such as eczema and psoriasis

- Respiratory problems, such as asthma, cough, and congestion

How Aromatherapy Is Used To Feel Good

Aromatherapy is also becoming widely used solely for the pleasure of the scents essential oils emanate. Essential oils are often found in cosmetics: perfume, skin care, and hair care products. They are also used in cleaning products as many plants have natural anti-fungal, anti-bacterial, and anti-viral properties to help protect the plant from bacteria and diseases other botanical benefits essential oils take advantage of. Essential oil fragrances have even been used by the tobacco industry.

While many essential oils are beneficial for the skin and hair, and while many essential oils are efficient solutions for cleaning and killing bacteria, these oils are also used for the aromatic pleasure they convey that is, their scents make people feel good.

In fact, there are essential oils that are believed to have aphrodisiac qualities. You might read in many an article that a drop of lavender or patchouli placed on the "pulse points" or on the "most kissable spots" of the body will help seduce the one you love. While essential oils are broadly used for their medicinal purposes, they are perhaps even more widely used for the feel-good properties that they emanate. Essential oils can be:

• Uplifting – bergamot and grapefruit

• Playful – sweet orange

• Calming – frankincense and tangerine

• Soporific – lavender

• Amorous – cinnamon leaf

• Energizing – peppermint and lemon

• Memory and concentration enhancing – rosemary and eucalyptus

What Is A Carrier Oil?

For topical application of essential oils, aromatherapy practitioners will always tell you to use a carrier oil, such as jojoba oil, argan oil, or coconut oil. Most experts, however, agree that there are some oils deemed safe to use on the skin (such as cedarwood, tea tree oil, frankincense, and lavender), but there are still a few who suggest using even these oils with a carrier oil. Suffice to say, carrier oils are extremely important because of the potency of essential oils.

Like essential oils, carrier oils are extracted from plants, but, unlike essential oils (apart from almond and nutmeg oils), they are usually made from seeds, nuts, and kernels, the fatty parts of the plant. For this reason, they don't have the intense aromas that essential oils do. They function to dilute the essential oili.e., to "carry" the essential oil before it is applied to your body or your face. They are the base (often called the "base oil") of your essential oil blend.

Although carrier oils each hold their own therapeutic values, their real principle healing and restorative benefits are attributed to their nourishing skin properties. And while most often carrier oils are mentioned for topical safety purposes, the primary reason they are used, again, is because they are so nourishing for the skin. Carrier oils are chosen because they are great moisturizers, and all of them can be used on their own for their restorative skin properties.

What Carrier Oils Are Commonly Used?

Just as essential oils can be combined to target certain symptoms or to discover a pleasant fragrance, so too can carrier oils be combined in an essential oil mixture in fact, it is sometimes advised. For instance, castor oil is a powerful emollient, but it is considered too thick and sticky to be used without being diluted with other carrier oils. Here is a list of some commonly used carrier oils:

- Argan Oil

Having a faint nutty and citrusy smell, argan oil is full of vitamin E and essential fatty acids. It nourishes skin and reduces inflammation. Argan oil can act as a face wash or a face moisturizer because it dissolves quickly and does not leave grease or oil behind. Argan oil has a shelf life of about two years.

- Avocado Oil

Having an earthy, nutty scent, avocado oil nourishes skin and promotes cell regeneration. It is deeply moisturizing and can be used as a cleanser. Avocado oil has a shelf life of about one year.

- Cocoa Butter

Having a chocolaty smell, cocoa butter helps to restore dry, cracked, and aging skin. It is rich in vitamin E, nourishing, and moisturizing. Cocoa butter has a shelf life of about one year.

- Coconut Oil

Having a tropical sweet smell, coconut oil can penetrate skin quicker than most other oils. It soothes dry skin and reduces inflammation, irritation, and itchiness. Coconut oil has a shelf life of about two years.

- Fractionated Coconut Oil

A scentless oil, fractionated coconut oil is a (naturally) refined version of coconut oil. It is a lightweight, hydrating moisturizer that quickly absorbs into the skin. It has a shelf life of five or more years.

- Jojoba Oil

Having a faint sweet smell, jojoba oil is used as a carrier oil because of its similarity to "sebum," a natural oil that the skin produces. It is a nourishing oil for either gentle or dry skin. Jojoba oil has an almost indefinite shelf life.

- Castor Oil

Some people say castor oil smells like its consistency: thick and oily. The smell can be tamed with a little essential oil. Still, castor oil is one of the best oils for any kind of skin condition: eczema, psoriasis, dermatitis. Because of its thick consistency, only about ten percent of castor oil is suggested for a carrier oil mix that will be massaged over large areas of the skin. It has a shelf life of about one year and should be refrigerated.

How To Make A Topical Essential Oil Mix

A good rule of thumb when making a carrier oil/essential oil mix is to add 1 to 3 percent essential oil to your chosen amount of carrier oil. To make a 1 percent dilution, add 5 to 6 drops of essential oil to every ounce (30 ml) of carrier oil. Then, just double (10 to 12 drops) and triple (15 to 18 drops) this as needed to make 2 and 3 percent dilutions, respectively.

• A 1 percent or less dilution is recommended for facial massages and for people with sensitive skin.

• A 2 percent dilution is recommended for daily use.

• A 3 percent dilution is recommended for health problems, such as sore muscle pain, but this should only be used for a short time.

The percentage can be increased, and often people that are used to wearing strong perfumes will find a 2 percent dilution a little weak at first. However, many people adjust to the strength of the scent and notice that it enhances over time.

Using Aromatherapy With A Diffuser

A diffuser is the most common and simplest way to use essential oils. A diffuser allows the oil or combination of oils you choose to be suspended in the air for hours, providing the physical or emotional benefits that you crave, receiving the feel-good effects you desire, or simply making a room smell good or free of air-borne pathogens. In order to use a diffuser, follow the manufacturer's instructions because there are many different kinds of diffusers. Choose a diffuser that is easy to use.

Diffusing uplifting oils such as lemon or tangerine can help create a cheerful atmosphere. Diffusing relaxing oils such as lavender or bergamot can help create a calming atmosphere. Diffusing anti-bacterial oils such as eucalyptus or tea tree can help clear the room of air-borne pathogens. Diffusing any of these oils, or a mixture of your choosing, will freshen the air and help clear the room of any bad odors.

Using Aromatherapy By Direct Inhalation

Place a couple drops in the palm of your hand and rub your hands together. Cup your hands over nose and mouth, then take 3 to 5 deep inhalations. Afterwards, give yourself at least 3 minutes to relax before continuing with whatever task you were doing. This method should only be practiced with certain oils and hands should be kept away from the eyes. For safe inhalation, 1 to 3 drops of essential oils can be placed on a cloth, a cotton ball, a handkerchief, or, if there is nothing else at hand, a folded paper towel.

Using Aromatherapy In A Bath

Mix 3 to 6 drops of essential oils with a carrier oil and add to a bath while the warm water is running, keeping most of the oils from floating to the top. A bath with essential oils allows you to receive not only the benefits of skin penetration but also the benefits of inhalation. Even better, the carrier oil in the bath water will moisturize your skin.

Using Aromatherapy With A Compress

Add 4 or 5 drops of essential oils to a bowl of hot or cold water. Fold the towel and lay it gently on the water for absorption. Then, wring out the excess water. Place the compress on the sore area and cover with a bandage. Remove the compress when it is no longer cold or hot. Repeat as necessary.

Using Aromatherapy In Unscented Facial And Body Lotions

Just as you would do with any carrier oil, add between 1 to 3 percent dilution to every 1 ounce of unscented cream or oil. Use only 1 to 2 percent for facial creams and for people with delicate skin. See how your skin reacts, then raise the dilution rate. Remember to mix well.

What Are Top, Middle, And Base Notes?

Each essential oil is classified as a top, a middle, or a base notes. Not every blend needs to contain each note, but a good smelling blend usually contains all three. Top, middle, and base notes are determined by the length of time it takes for an individual oil to evaporate. Using all three notes in an essential oil mixture allows the blend to be layered and cohesive.

Top notes are the first oils that you smell in a diffused or topical blend and they are the first oils to evaporate. Top notes usually have a fresh yet strong smell. Citrus oils such as bergamot, grapefruit, lime, and sweet orange fall into this category. Middle notes usually have warmer smells. They include oils such as rosemary and lavender. Base notes generally have deep, earthy smells, such as frankincense and patchouli. Base notes take the longest to detect but their presence also lingers the longest.

The practice of blending essential oils is the reason that aromatherapy will always be described as something between an art and a science. A masseuse or holistic practitioner might prepare a blend for a particular therapeutic purpose, but they also want the blend to have a pleasant fragrance.

How Do I Choose The Essential Oils That Are Right For Me?

Many companies claim that their oils are "pure" or "medical grade." However, these terms aren't universally defined and therefore hold little weight. Given that they're products of an unregulated industry, the ⬚uality and composition of essential oils can vary greatly.

Keep the following tips in mind to choose only high-quality oils:

•   Purity: Find an oil that contains only aromatic plant compounds, without additives or synthetic oils. Pure oils usually list the plant's botanical name (such as Lavandula officinalis) rather than terms like "essential oil of lavender."

•   Quality: True essential oils are the ones that have been changed the least by the extraction process. Choose a chemical-free essential oil that has been extracted through distillation or mechanical cold pressing.

•   Reputation: Purchase a brand with a reputation for producing high-⬚uality products.

You don't necessarily need research to tell you which essential oils make you feel good. Many smells are very personal. For instance, some people find patchouli seductive while others are turned off by it.

Our sense of smell is tied to the limbic system, an area of the brain that processes emotion (it's actually described as "the emotional center of the brain"). The limbic system is also an area where long-term memories are stored. Emotions and memories are deeply connected to our sense of smell. For this reason, some scents attract and others repel. While many scents encourage common responses, many individual scents induce very individual reactions. If the first time you smelled roses was at a funeral, then rose oil might not remind you of love, but of loss. So, it is best to learn how your body responds to each different oil.

To find out whether you like an oil or not, it is best to put a couple of drops on a napkin or cloth and then smell the material from about 6 inches away. This is a better method then trying to take a whiff straight from the bottle.

Remember too: Different essential oils have different effects in different situations. If work is over and you need to relax, then lavender or bergamot might be the right oil to diffuse. If you need energy to get through work, then peppermint or lemon might be a better oil to have on hand.

How Do I Use Essential Oils Safely?

Essential oils might be natural, but they are potent and powerful. A huge amount of plant material is used to make a very small amount of oil. For instance, it takes about two hundred kilograms of lavender flowers to produce one kilogram of lavender essential oil. It takes about four dozen roses to produce a single drop of rose oil. So, these highly concentrated oils deserve our respect.

- Irritation and allergic reactions

It is rare, but some people have allergic reactions (also called "sensitivity") to certain essential oils. Some people also develop irritation when they use oils topically. To find out whether someone is allergic or sensitive to a certain oil, a "patch test" is often suggested. There are critics who believe that a patch test will not clearly show whether someone has an allergy to the oil or, conversely, who believe that a patch test might actually cause irritation. However, these same critics haven't offered many other ways to test whether an essential oil can cause sensitivity or irritation.

Here is how to perform a patch test: Mix 1 drop of essential oil into 1 tsp (5 mL) of carrier oil. Place a small amount of the mixture on the crook of your elbow or the back of your arm, and cover the applied area with a large bandage. Wait twenty-four hours to see whether there is a reaction.

• Near the eyes

Keep essential oils away from your eyes. If an oil gets in your eyes, irrigate your eyes with milk or with a vegetable oil, and gently wipe the irritated eye with a soft tissue.

• Photosensitivity

Most citrus-based oils can cause photosensitivity (often depending on whether they are distilled or expressed), meaning that, if a citrus-based essential oil is applied topically, it can irritate, redden, or darken the pigmentation of the skin when exposed to direct sunlight within twelve hours of application.

- Ingesting

Many websites, and some books, will suggest putting a drop or two of essential oils in your water or will give advice on cooking with essential oils. However, most books written on aromatherapy will advise against any ingestion of essential oils unless you have first spoken to a doctor or an aromatherapist. That said, some essential oils can be ingested in small amount, but you should be discerning and check your sources.

- Children

Just as you shouldn't keep your aspirin lying around in a place where children can get hold of them, so too should you not keep essential oils where children can come into contact with them. Some people recommend that children can use most essential oil mixtures at a 1 percent dilution rate or at half the strength that an adult would use. It is always recommended that a holistic care professional be consulted before using essential oils topically on a child under twelve. If a child accidently drinks the oil, give them milk immediately (to dilute the oil), then take them to a hospital. Essential oil products that come pre-mixed are made with adults in mind.

- Pregnant women

It is often recommended that pregnant women should use 1 percent dilution when using essential oils topically. It is also often suggested that pregnant women should not use essential oils during their first trimester. However, one thing is certain, pregnant women should definitely avoid some essential oils, such as sage oil, because they are emmenagogues (they stimulate or increase menstrual flow). It is best to look up which essential oils fall into this category.

As a final note, don't let safety precautions keep you from experimenting with essential oils. Essential oils are much safer than most of the drugs you store in your medicine cabinet. The biggest fear is that a child or a pet might confuse their sweet scent with something that can be consumed.

CPSIA information can be obtained
at www.ICGtesting.com
Printed in the USA
BVHW041351160821
614506BV00016B/683